For Larry,

With gratitude for support and help in
ministry during our years at St. Timothy's.

Ted +

SUCCESS AND THE CLERGY

Success

and the

Clergy

by

Ted McConnell

PORTLAND•OREGON
INKWATERPRESS.COM

*Scan this QR Code
to learn more about
this title.*

Publisher: Inkwater Press | www.inkwaterpress.com
Paperback ISBN-13 978-1-62901-259-9 | ISBN-10 1-62901-259-9

    McConnell, Theodore, 1938-
      Success and the clergy / by Ted McConnell.
      pages cm
      LCCN 2015907900
      ISBN 978-1-62901-259-9 (pbk.)

      1. Clergy. 2. Success. 3. Leadership. I. Title.

    BV660.3.M345 2015   253
                    QBI15-600111

Printed in the U.S.A.

1 3 5 7 9 10 8 6 4 2

In Memory Of

Molly Cochran McConnell
1941–2013

A Beautiful and Kind Soul
With God's Grace and Mercy May She
R. I. P.

Table of Contents

Preface ix

Chapter 1. Hearing the Call and Being Called 1

Chapter 2. Professing the Call, Living the Calling 13

Chapter 3. Success and the Sacred Calling 29

Chapter 4. All Things To All People? 43

Chapter 5. God's Calling and the Churches 49

Chapter 6. In Season and Out of Season 65

Chapter 7. Having the Mind and Spirit 73

About the Author 81

Preface

THIS BOOK IS FOR ALL CLERGY WHO HAVE BEEN CALLED BY GOD, THOSE struggling with God's call, those seeking to understand this call including the people in the pews.

What is presented here is one distinctive perspective of the sacred call and calling. It is a perspective that is clearly drawn and etched against other perspectives, set in the midst of a society that for the most part disdains and dismisses this calling. It is a perspective based upon the conviction that obedience to God's call and faithfulness to this calling is of utmost significance whether society so judges it or not. At various points I shall try to make clear where and how this calling has to stand in judgment upon the world and the churches and why it must do so.

Even to speak of the clergy vocation with the words *call and calling* is, I suppose, to mark this perspective as out of joint with the times. I persist in using those words in the face of that judgment because I believe that the essence of this particular vocation is embodied in those words *call and calling*. The theological substance of that conviction is developed in what follows.

I also believe that this call and calling is sacred because it comes from God and so there can be no compromises about its origin and identity. Clergy and churches that find their identity elsewhere are wolves in sheep's clothing who seek to claim the calling for themselves. In doing so they are subverting the calling. Those of us in this calling know that subversion all too well, although it is seldom mentioned or described. This book aims to expose the wolves, showing just how harmful they are to the proclamation of the Gospel. This book is also a reformer's book in Luther's sense of reform—to re-form ourselves and the churches that we serve. Once again it is time to discern more clearly what is involved in hearing God's call and what shall be required of us if we are to be faithful to that call.

Finally, I believe a minister's calling is to bear the burdens of others—emotional, spiritual, physical. All the burdens of others whatever they may be today and tomorrow.

How is that achieved? Only with our Lord's help. I know that I could have done much more during the past fifty-two years. And what I have done I should have done better.

TED MCCONNELL

SUCCESS AND THE CLERGY

CHAPTER 1

Hearing the Call and Being Called

THE LATE WILL CAMPBELL TOLD HOW HIS DECISION TO BECOME A preacher took place at age seven after he was baptized. "He thought he intended to be a preacher because he had been called to be one."[1] His intention was not because his parents or his family or his preacher or anyone else told him to be a preacher. No, he would become a preacher because he was called to preach the Lord's message in every season and every place he lived.

Being called to the ministry has always been a strange experience for Christians and Jews. How do you know that you've been called? When were you called anyway? Where were you? How can you be so certain about it? Moses protested from time to time about his call. So did Isaiah, Jeremiah, Job, and St. Paul. And over the years and centuries many others have tried to avoid and evade this call. How do you avoid becoming a fraud or a charlatan or a fool? Of course many times in our lives we may be fools for the Lord; however, we hope that is different than being a dumb fool and that we shall know the difference.

---

1   Will D. Campbell, *Forty Acres and a Goat*. Atlanta: Peachtree Publishers, 1986, p. 2.

Hearing the Call

Whether one has heard God's call to the sacred calling is often a perplexing matter for us and frequently a matter of dispute within ourselves or among churches. What has one heard? Has there been an authentic call or something else? Wish fulfillment, self-delusion, or a self-seeking drive to become god? There is ample opportunity for confusion in this business of being called to this calling, and the old jibe is well taken about the young man who presented himself for ordination, testifying that while out in the fields planting corn he saw the letters *P C* written across the sky. These he took to mean *Preach Christ*, but after hearing him preach, one pastor remarked, "I think the *P C* meant plant corn!"

It is sometimes confusing for us because so many calls and claims that have nothing to do with the Christian calling can impinge upon our hearing. These have to be sorted out and clearly identified for what they are. In this age as in any age a multitude of ideologies present themselves as worthy objects for our loyalty and commitment. Often these claim to be part of the Gospel when in fact they are something else masquerading under the Gospel's name. The calls to practice a personal religion and morality have become particularly prominent in our time. These calls stand for an individualism that defines all religious beliefs and values as expressions of individual preference and nothing else. As identified in one study of American religion, the sovereignty of the individual leads to a religious populism that "implies fluid standards, diversity in ideas and styles, changing definitions of common beliefs, and core practices that can unify and integrate the largest majority."[1] In other words, a majority vote decides all matters and in a time of fiercely guarded individualism, this means the lowest common denominator necessary to gain a majority. Then there are the "power" calls of our age that lure many

---

1   Wade Clark Roof and William McKinney, *American Mainline Religion*. New Brunswick: Rutgers University Press, 1987, p. 249.

people into supposedly religious vocations where they pursue the amassing of greater and greater power over other people. The pursuit of power has become a trademark of the churches, about which I shall have more to say later.

Whatever the ideologies and their calls, it is crucial that those who would serve God not confuse those calls and claims with the call of Jesus Christ and His Gospel. Whether we discern that difference shall make all the difference for us and our calling. There are a multitude of gods set before us at all times and it is the nature of our human freedom to be able to choose our loyalties. For some, including some in the churches, there is an easy movement off into ego-centric beliefs and actions and the delusions of ego-mania. For others, there is genuine confusion about what, if any, call can be heard and heeded. And for some, there is a clear, direct call that holds no distortions or confusion. To hear clearly and heed such a call is a mark of our calling. Indeed, it might be said that those who are beset by unending confusion, doubt, and despair probably have as clear an indication as any that they have not been called. Those who have been called, like Abraham and Moses and Isaiah and John, Peter, and Paul, know that they have been called.

What moves us to hear the call is best left to God. At the same time we need to recognize that God may choose to use some mighty strange and unusual ways to bring people to hear the call. This point has been made for me again and again with compelling clarity and wonderful humor in reading the novels and stories of J.F. Powers. The ways of God in calling Father Urban in *Morte D'Urban*, Bishop John Dullinger in *Look How the Fish Live*, and Father Joe in *Wheat That Springeth Green* show just how much God is in charge of this calling business.[2] Those ways are not usually our ways, not by our reckoning anyway. But then we need to remind ourselves that we are not God and so our way of seeing is not always very clear or

---

2   J.F. Powers, *Morte D'Urban*. Garden City: Doubleday and Co., 1962; *Look How the Fish Live*. New York City: Knopf, 1975; *Wheat That Springeth Green*. New York City: Knopf, 1988.

perfect. God chooses ways and means that often make little sense to us. Whether it is done to break through all the competing din or for some other purposes, we have a big enough job hearing and heeding the call without trying to have the last word on why the call has come as it has or where it shall take us. Rather, what we need to strive for is a restless, ceaseless listening to hear the call whenever and however it may come to us. And if we have heard that call, then it is likely that we shall try to avoid it for as long as possible.

Avoiding the Call

Trying to avoid God's call is a familiar part of our Judeo-Christian heritage. There is an almost instinctive reluctance and certainly a human fear of such an awesome task. To be called to speak for God and lead people to God evokes fear and trembling. Who of us is equal to this task or worthy of it? That was Jacob's first response and he wrestled long and hard before heeding God's call. Resistance was also Moses' response to God. Who am I? (Ex. 3) "I am slow of speech and of tongue." In fact, Moses resisted God's call so long that the Lord was angry with him. (Ex. 4:10-15) Resistance was also Jeremiah's first response and even more so that of the ever reluctant Jonah. Isaiah was ever so fretful about preaching God's Word and described himself as having unclean lips until an angel purged them. So too Jesus' disciples were frequently hesitating and reluctant followers who had trouble getting their call straight and heeding it.

Perhaps there also is a strong impulse to avoid God's call because somehow we know what a costly thing it shall be for us to heed that call. The fear of such a costly way and all that it entails surely prompts us to try avoiding the call. Like Moses and Isaiah and Jeremiah, we are not equal to the task and the calling. So, pray Lord, send another! That is often our response and our first inclination. But then what shall we do when the Lord will have no other and not send another in our place?

Heeding the Call

There is no getting around it, finally. If we're called we've got to heed the call and better sooner than later. The only reason for heeding this call is because we've been called by God. Nothing else will do; we cannot escape it or avoid it and no other will be sent in our place. For us, like the young Samuel, the response is, "Speak, for thy servant hears." (I Sam. 3:10)

To heed God's call is to begin to accept a lifelong calling. It is to take up a responsibility as one who stands for God wherever we happen to find ourselves. Committing ourselves to this calling is unlike any other commitment for it demands our complete and undivided loyalty and devotion. Moreover, this call practically guarantees that we shall have a difficult and tormented way in this life. Indeed, Jesus promised that those who hear His call and accept this calling will suffer all kinds of dangers, persecutions, and downfalls in their lifetime. This is not a call to well-being, success, and prosperity in this life. Those who have heard this call simply heed it in spite of all its promised perils because it is God's call to them. Like Isaiah, we have heard God's voice saying, "Whom shall I send, and who will go for us?" And somehow, instinctively, we are confident of our reply: "Here am I! Send me." (Isa. 6:8)

Called by the Church

We live in a society made up of institutions and for most of us the decision to heed God's call will be lived out through the institution of the church. Indeed, for most the call comes by way of a church or in some part through the influence of a church. This is what Martin Luther described as the "mediated call" as contrasted to that of the Apostles, who were called directly by Jesus, and the Prophets, who were called by God. Now, in these later days, the call most often seems to come by some means of a church, although God just might choose some other means. Certainly the churches need to remain open to that possibility, indeed far more open than many of them have been! Ordinations, coming by way of the churches, are regarded as the sign and seal of a valid call in our age. Ordination has become part of the church's means for validating an inward call. Historically the churches have regarded themselves as our Lord's designated agents in confirming the call and overseeing the calling. And all those who believe that they are called, and are seeking to fulfill their calling in a church, must obtain that church's recognition and approval before taking up the ministry.

What constitutes a valid call and a life worthy of ordination is determined for us by the churches, operating through structures and procedures and all kinds of processes. It is here that the testing of one's call begins. The variety of procedures developed by churches to determine who shall be ordained is almost as diverse and numerous as the denominations of churches. However, for the greater portion, the path to ordination now involves a variety of evaluations and evaluators, usually several times during a period of preparation and education. Many denominations now begin with parish committees that decide who shall be recommended as "candidates." As those selected then move along toward ordination, all the evaluations and testing come into operation. In some denominations a diocesan or synod-wide ministry committee made up of laity and clergy carries the major responsibility for administering the entire procedure and deciding who shall be ordained. It is here that some of the gravest and most vexing theological problems have emerged in our time concerning the call.

Right away we have to ask whether the churches ought ever to turn to such committees and procedures. Can committees and commissions with their voting procedures and decision-making ever be squared with the Scriptures and the Gospel of Christ? To move the question of "qualification" and who is qualified back to its beginning point, what qualifies or justifies the appointment of any such group for this task? We need to face it: there is no qualification and no justification. To make committees and commissions "on ministry" the gatekeepers to ordination and the evaluators of the call is neither justified or validated by Scripture. Moreover, it is bad theology and even worse ecclesiology.

Increasingly it can be observed that committees or commissions on ministry have become ideological battlegrounds occupied by a diversity of special interest groups that inhabit most of the churches. Under these circumstances ideologies of the right or left and countless isms supplant the Gospel and subvert the Gospel while calling their program the gospel. One step toward ending this apostasy would be to eliminate any structure or procedure that fosters it.

Finally, whatever else they may do, the churches have no justification and much to regret and fear from delivering the evaluation of God's call into the hands of any committees or vote taking bodies. In these matters the only clear Scriptural warrants are for a line of sacred calling begun by our Lord's calling of His disciples, by His handing over of the calling to them in succession, and by their casting of lots for the leadership. No committees; no commissions! No secular "experts" or evaluators or examiners! Thomas Oden, a Methodist pastor, has summarized this historic position in a succinct and comprehensive way:

> The classical ecumenical consensus affirmed by Catholics and Protestants alike is that duly authorized ministers are entrusted with the selection process that continues the apostolic tradition in each new generation. Although there are some traditions that would differ on this point, as a rule the gift of sacred ministry has not been given or legitimated by populist standards. ... The one objective above all to which ordained ministry is committed is the continuity and maintenance of the apostolic tradition.[1]

---

1   Thomas C. Oden, *Becoming a Minister*. New York City: Crossroad Publishing Co., 1987, pp. 21–22.

The sacred calling is passed down from generation to generation and age to age by those called and dedicated to this calling. Whenever that calling is placed under the determination and control of vote taking and gathering, it is compromised and usually abandoned.

Another testing of the calling that has appeared in our time among the churches is an increasing reliance upon the evaluations of secular "experts" in psychology, psychiatry, and medicine. Candidates for ordination are tested and evaluated once, twice, or yearly during their time of education and preparation. Seminarians are examined and re-examined and commissions and ordaining councils have increasingly placed their trust in these secular trades for judgments about the fitness of candidates and the authenticity of their calls.

Profound theological objections must be raised against such trends and procedures. To see churches placing such naive and intense trust in secular ideologies is a cause for decisive judgment against them. The cause for judgment is that in so doing our Lord's Gospel is sold out to worldly ideologies and practices. Moreover, these practices have little or nothing to do with this sacred calling. Dr. Robert Coles, the noted research psychiatrist, has put this matter plainly in challenging the decisions of seminaries, ordinations councils, and bishops that want candidates who are determined to be psychologically fit and healthy. Perhaps there are some occasions when a psychiatric evaluation is interesting or useful, but says Coles, "there are many psychiatrists who have no real understanding of what a religious vocation is about; and some of us are narrow-minded, smug, possessed of our own sectarian, ideological faith—hence the last persons in the world who ought to be writing letters of 'evaluation' to bishops." Moreover, Coles adds, psychological ideas of normal and deviant are frequently thinly disguised value judgments that support a particular ideology. He then concludes with what should be the decisive word on this practice: Having frequently been asked by bishops and various church agencies to participate in evaluations of candidates, "No one has ever asked me what qualification—what understanding of the spiritual life—I have to fill out these various forms. All I need do is affix the letters M.D. after my name, indicate my psychiatric affiliation, and my words are accepted as thoughtful and helpful."[1]

In following Coles, Richard Neuhaus wisely pointed out that the Christian tradition has within itself all the necessary "standards" and "norms" for evaluating the call and the calling.

> The cardinal virtues of prudence, justice, fortitude and temperance; the sins of pride, envy, sloth, despair—are not these ever so much more textured and rich and comprehensive than is the jargon of our therapeutic society? It is no advance to "explain" the meaning of love by translating I Corinthians 13 into the professional prattle of the clinic. It is at least unbecoming and probably blasphemous to norm the Christian life by the criteria of the therapeutic.[2]

If anyone is seeking additional standards of evaluation, then those of Scripture, tradition, the Creeds, and the ministry of Word and Sacrament ought to be the standard. It is shameful that any church should need to be reminded of these standards or recalled to them. Nevertheless that is now the situation which we face among the churches. It is blasphemous for any church or church officer to evaluate the Christian calling by the secular standards of psychology, psychiatry, medicine, or any ideology. Handing over the church's calling process to the ways and means of any worldly standards is to deny our Lord and His Gospel. In spite of any secular standards or judgments, those who have been called know that they have been called and can testify to that call. The measure of their calling is that provided by St. Paul: "For necessity is laid upon me.

---

1   Robert Coles, "New Forms of the Sin of Pride," in *The New Review of Books and Religion,* December, 1977, p. 3.

2   Richard John Neuhaus, *Freedom for Ministry.* San Francisco: Harper and Row, 1979, p. 76.

Woe to me if I do not preach the gospel! For if I do this of my own will, I have a reward, but if not of my own will, I am entrusted with a commission." (1 Cor. 9) So let all the churches heed this way and get their houses in order, getting themselves out of the hands of all the secular experts and back to the heart and mind of Christ.

The Devil's Call

For as long as there have been churches and clergy they have been beset with another kind of call that frequently is confused with God's call. The Devil's call is a seductive and ingenious one whose intent is to turn churches and clergy against the divine call. This campaign of "disinformation," to use a modern political expression, leads directly into a theological and ecclesiastical wilderness of mirrors where every belief and commitment becomes suspect. The ultimate aim, of course, is the "turning" or converting of all believers and the destruction of Christian belief.

Luther analyzed the Devil's threat to the churches and the calling in a 1532 letter, "Infiltrating and Clandestine Preachers." For us the theological foundation and structure of that letter is more important than its historical context regarding certain Anabaptist teaching in the town of Eisenach. What Luther had to say, in brief, was that the marks of the Devil's infiltration of the churches were likely to appear at any time and especially among clergy seduced by the Devil's call. The marks of such infiltration are a preference for secretiveness and stealth by which the Devil aims to dislodge Christ's Gospel and secretly subvert it; a stealing of churches and preachers for the Devil's purposes; and a fostering of chaos and rebellion, all carried out under the guise of Christianity.[1]

The Devil's call is always the most dangerous threat to God's call and calling, for it strikes from within. The clergy are the Devil's

1   Martin Luther, *Luther's Works*. Philadelphia: Fortress Press, 1958, vol. 40, pp. 383–394.

preferred targets in a continuous battle for the mind and soul of the churches. Recognizing the Devil's infiltration ought to be of utmost concern to the churches although it has seldom turned out that way. What is needed? Luther's sage advice was that we must press the matter of the call continuously: "Who has sent you?"[2] What we claim as our call and the one who has sent us marks us and our calling. Whenever and wherever it involves stealth, subversion, chaos, and rebellion, it bears the marks of the Devil. His call is the siren song of countless worldly plots and plans that overrun the churches and entice clergy. In our age these schemes can be seen especially in a newfound trust in secular values and outlooks, in the pursuit of success and power, and in the compromising of faith in our call and the One whom we are called to serve. As Richard Neuhaus aptly described it, what is taking place in many churches is an "attempt to replace the Gospel itself with an ideology for social transformation, which we then call the gospel."[3]

In response to the subverting of the Gospel from within, again and again it has to be asked of us: "Who sent you?" And it is only to the degree that we can answer with a clear conscience, "Christ Jesus is His name, from age to age the same, and He will win the battle" that we are faithful servants of God's call and calling.

Called by God

Those called by God are called to a calling unlike any other vocation or profession or living. God's call is to abandon all other calls in order to serve Him in the name of His incarnate Son, Jesus Christ, professing Christ's Gospel in His Holy Name. Of course this is an impossible calling for any of us by ourselves. But we are not called by ourselves or for ourselves. We are called by God

---

2   *Ibid.*, pp. 384, 386.
3   Richard John Neuhaus, *The Catholic Moment*. San Francisco: Harper and Row, 1987, p. 227.

to heed His call on His terms. That is why it is so important to press the requirement that we forsake ourselves and all self-seeking. There is no place in God's calling for those who serve themselves or promote themselves. The call of this calling is to serve God in His blessed Son. Anything else, anything less, is not this calling.

The call of the Devil and the call to self-aggrandizement are sometimes separate, sometimes intertwined with each other. Whatever the case, they stand in opposition to God's call, even as they masquerade under its name. Let no one be fooled by all the disguises and trickery. Press again and again the questions, who sent you and by what authority are you doing these things? Those called by God know by whom they have been called and will be able to give a good account of themselves. They will show that they stand for the Lord by always standing aside, giving Him the honor and glory. They will profess Christ crucified, risen, ascended into heaven and coming again at the end of all time. Those so called know that they have no other choice and can be no other, for they have been called by God.

CHAPTER 2

Professing the Call, Living the Calling

MORE THAN FIFTY YEARS AGO THE WIDELY RESPECTED EVANGELICAL and Reformed Church clergyman and Yale professor H. Richard Niebuhr described what he perceived to be an "emerging new conception of the ministry," which he named the "pastoral director."[1] Niebuhr carefully depicted a fundamental change from historic concepts of the clergy as priest, preacher, prophet, and evangelist to one of a multi-purpose director of the church's ministry. This new formative image and model for clergy was said to involve "the administration of a community that is directed toward the whole purpose of the church, namely the increase among men of the love of God and neighbor; for the church is becoming the minister and its 'minister' is its servant, directing it in its service."[2]

What Niebuhr did not say and probably would not have agreed to, but which has become increasingly clear in the intervening years, is that this emerging new conception of the ministry has led to a

---

1   H. Richard Niebuhr, *The Purpose of the Church and the Ministry*. New York: Harper and Row, 1956, see especially pp. 48–94.

2   *Ibid.*, p. 83.

subtle but monumental theological and practical shift away from God's call and calling to the church's call and ministry. The two are not always or necessarily the same, contrary to all expectations. In Chapter 5 the meaning and implications of this difference will be discussed more fully, but at the moment it is important to recognize the immense significance and continuing impact of such a radical change. The beginnings of this new way of seeing the calling that Niebuhr so aptly identified embodied a pronounced shift away from the Biblical foundations of prophet, priest, evangelist, and teacher to institutional and administrative foundations. The church became the minister and the clergy are now called to be its pastoral directors and administrators. The new image embodied another theological change of major proportions, which was a reversal of the created order of things. In the order of creation, the Gospel creates the church, but with this reversal the church creates the gospel. This new image of the clergy calling marks an abandonment of God's call and calling; it is the move from a God-centered to an institution-centered ministry.

This new conception of ministry has grown and developed in many ways in the more than five decades since Niebuhr's descriptive identification. A plethora of images and models of the church's purpose and ministry have been advocated as the clergy calling has been endlessly redefined and remolded into a variety of secular forms. Now we live in a time characterized by strident competing advocates of various "ministries." Seminarians and clergy are pressed on every side by competing images as Niebuhr's relatively inclusive "pastoral director" has been eclipsed by more specialized and specialist models.

The Pastoral Specialists

In recent years clergy have been urged to think of themselves as directors and managers of institutions and "volunteer organizations," as "conflict managers," "counselors," "enablers," and dynamic group life "facilitators." The jargon-laden designs and theories of industrial and social psychology, business management, social work, community organizing, and political action movements have been increasingly appropriated by the churches. Seminary curricula have been considerably modified and in some instances the new methods and models are predominant. The age of pastoral specialists is upon us. And with this age have come substantial changes in the commitments and values of clergy.

The shift from a God-centered to an institution-centered ministry has generated a growing array of secular tools and gospels. Explicit, often frenetic and even pathetic imitating of secular methods and vocabularies is everywhere apparent in the churches now. This has been accompanied by an obsession with costs and benefits: What will this action cost me? What benefits will it bring to me? As Robert Bellah has commented, this new narcissism is a product, perhaps the only product and result of the widespread influence of psychological and therapeutic ideologies.[1] Clergy are urged to obtain training in this or that technique or "school," becoming specialists in one or another of those secular trades. Psychological and therapeutic approaches to individual, family, or community problems are said to engender and promote change, more "flexible and pluralistic views," and more "functional behavior." Taken on the surface and at face value, all these developments might be regarded as simply the latest and most trendy creations of restless minds and souls that lack a clear spiritual and theological commitment. However, much more is involved here, especially in terms of the results and consequences for professing God's call and living the calling.

Accommodation and Abandonment

The new age of the pastoral specialists has brought damage and destruction to our call and calling. The move from a God-centered

---

1   Robert N. Bellah, et al., *Habits of the Heart*. San Francisco: Harper and Row, 1986, see especially chapter 5.

to an institution-centered ministry has been foremost but by no means the only destruction. The new images and forms of ministry have also involved an accommodation to society and the culture that is marked by an adoption of secular ideologies and methods that entail abandonment of the Gospel. This is not to say that every accommodation or even some borrowing from the world and its secular methods leads to the Gospel's abandonment, but in this instance it has been so. It has been so because the commitments and values embedded in the methods, schools, and tools of this new age of pastoral specialists are not those of the Gospel. In them and by them the Gospel is either ignored or changed into something else. The understanding of God's call and calling has been drastically altered beginning with the move from a God-centered to an institution-centered concept of ministry. The standards of revelation and the Gospel have been replaced by the values of various secular ideologies including those of psychology, therapy, sociology, and business administration.

One evidence and result of this accommodation is a new understanding of religious belief. Religious belief is now said to be either "authoritarian," in which obedience is crucial, or "humanitarian," in which "self-realization" is the primary attribute. By implication, authoritarian is bad and to be avoided while humanitarian is good. For the most part, this humanitarian religion is nothing more or less than a secular humanism in which the values of change, progress, and selfish desires are paramount.

During a lengthy public career the psychologist Erich Fromm vigorously promoted the either/or choice of authoritarian versus humanitarian, and this has become widely accepted without much consideration being given to its hidden values and stereotypes. Whether obedience to God and humanitarian goals are necessarily contradictory and exclude each other is open to challenge and it is by no means certain that this way of seeing religion is valid or warranted. What is certain is that such an approach leads to a debunking of historic Christian belief while fostering a new kind of hedonism based upon the self. Self-realization, self-fulfillment, and self-gratification are the treasured standards and values of human-itarian ideology and the "triumph of the therapeutic" is its trade-mark. It is the opposite of the Gospel's teaching about denying the self and losing one's self for Christ's sake and the Gospel.[1]

Another evidence and result of accommodation to worldly standards and values is an abandonment of the three-fold ministry of preaching, teaching, and healing. With the embracing of pas-toral specialties modeled after the methods and tools of psychology and business administration has come a turning from preaching, teaching, and healing as the center and purpose of the clergy's calling. It is usually argued that the new specialties are simply con-temporary ways of proclaiming, teaching, and healing. However, what goes unexamined here are the values embodied in the new specialties and how these irrevocably alter the Christian message, transforming it into another ideology. There is a rather obvious deception here: the Gospel is replaced with an ideology which is then called the gospel. Nevertheless, that deception is practiced fervently by many within the churches.

One question that does not seem to be asked by many in the churches is, "When the Son of Man comes will He find faith on earth?" (Lk. 18:8) That is the question that defines the sacred calling and establishes its foundation and framework. The ques-tion is Christ's question to us; it all begins with Him and shall end with Him upon His return. In the meantime—the in-between time—it is left to us to preach, teach and heal *in His name.* Apart from this, abandonment of the Gospel is a certainty.

Called to What?

We are called to profess Jesus Christ as Lord and Savior of all,

---

1   See Philip Rieff, *The Triumph of the Therapeutic: Uses of Faith After Freud.* New York, NY: Harper & Row, 1966.

preaching, teaching, and baptizing in His name. Being called to this calling involves becoming prophet, priest, and pastor. It is, of course, an impossible calling and yet those called cannot hide from it or evade it. There is no better foundation for our call as prophets than that of God's calling of Samuel as told in I Samuel 3:1–20. The substance of the prophetic call is developed and amplified for us throughout the history and biographies of the prophets. It is a history that shows us exactly how we are called to proclaim and profess the Lord's Word to the world, in the world, against the world and its worldly standards. As prophets we are called to call the world to change and be transformed, rather than transforming the message and ourselves to "go along to get along." The clear word of Samuel in Eli's house, the plumb line of Amos, the unvarnished judgments of Isaiah, the vexing struggles of Jeremiah, the resounding call of Ezekiel to a faithless and unknowing people, and the amazing confrontations of Daniel show us the nature of our prophetic calling. Most of all, of course, we are given the substance of the prophetic calling by that one who was greater than any prophet, our Lord Jesus Christ. The prophetic message must be proclaimed and more often than not the proclaimer will encounter dispute and persecution because of the message delivered. The prophetic calling is a solitary and isolated existence that commits everything to the calling and the message.

The priestly and pastoral part of this sacred calling is just as demanding as the prophetic part. It involves our unreserved discipleship to the cross of Christ, a denial of self, a steadfast preaching of the Gospel, and an unwavering commitment to the eschatological promises of our Lord. To be called as pastors and preachers is to follow Jesus Christ. That is to profess His crucifixion, resurrection, and ascension, to teach His Gospel and proclaim His Lordship over the entire creation. To preach, teach, and baptize *in His name* and no other name throughout the world is our calling as priests and pastors. (See especially Mt. 28:16–20; Lk. 24:44–49; Jn. 20:19–23; Acts 1:4–8.)

One modern translation of the Book of Acts provides an especially clear summary of what we are called to: "And he commissioned us to carry the word and be the evidence that this Jesus has been established by God as the criterion for both the living and the dead. The whole Bible points to him—that everyone who bets his life on him received forgiveness for his sins, for Jesus' sake."[1] (Acts 10:42–43)

Our commission to carry the word and be the evidence puts us under a lifelong obligation to be faithful to God's call, to give up all self-interests and ambitions, and to steadfastly believe in God as revealed to us in Jesus Christ, serving Him only. The practice of our calling is the proclamation of Christ's Gospel in season and out of season. In being called we face a lifetime testing of our faithfulness, our self-sacrifice, and our believing service.

First, then, the testing of our faithfulness to our calling comes again and again in temptations to abandon it or exchange it for something else. Those temptations come from within ourselves by way of doubt and despair that we shall ever live up to our call and from outside by way of a multitude of forces and pressures in the churches and the world. The ranks of the clergy include those who once believed but no longer believe. Yet they remain, whether because of pride, greed, or fear, refusing to admit what is apparent to all. What such disbelieving clergy often resort to is developing another belief which they then call the gospel. The self-deception involved here is damaging and tragic enough in itself, but when it begins to influence others, then immense damage is inflicted upon the calling. Nowhere is this more harmful than in the hands of the church's leaders. Unnecessary and unjustified harm has been wrought upon countless clergy by the advocacies of unfaithful prelates. The beguiling trickery of disbelief masquerading under the church's name is lethal. Remaining faithful to God's call in the face of such forces requires unusual fortitude and conviction. But

---

1   Translation of Acts 10:42–43 by Clarence Jordan, *The Cotton Patch Version of Luke and Acts*. New York: Association Press, 1969.

most of all, God's grace is needed for us to remain faithful. To profess Jesus Christ as Lord and Savior clearly, simply, and without qualification is our call. In that definitive fourth chapter of 2 Corinthians, St. Paul tells us that this is the way of our calling: "We refuse to practice cunning or to tamper with God's word, but by the open statement of the truth we would commend ourselves to every man's conscience in the sight of God." (2 Cor. 4:2)

A second testing of us is that we are called to give up ourselves for the sake of Christ and His Gospel. Again, St. Paul shows us the way: "For what we preach is not ourselves, but Jesus Christ as Lord." (2 Cor. 4:5) Always, our solitary commitment is to God in Jesus Christ our Lord. For the disciples, serving God in following Jesus involved abandoning their trades and jobs because He called them. Even then, following Jesus was both an external and an internal matter: it involved not simply following Him around Galilee, but also completely changing one's internal life to fit Jesus' will and way. Self-renunciation was central to following Jesus. Here we can begin to perceive the personal meaning and implications of God's calling. Numerous events in the lives of the disciples show us that the demands of following Jesus were the absolute demands of giving up and giving away the self. Repeatedly in the Gospels it is made clear how difficult it was for any of the disciples to bring about that self-renunciation. Jesus' call to His disciples (and by explicit extension to all clergy) was simply: "Follow Me!" And as Jesus' ministry developed, it became apparent exactly what "Follow Me" involved. Not only did it involve self-renunciation, but as the persecution of Jesus increased, following Him meant becoming an outcast and ultimately a martyr. Jesus made clear the meaning and the cost of His call: "Whosoever will come after me, let him deny himself and take up his cross and follow me." (Mk. 8:34 KJV) There we have it! Being called by Jesus means a life of self-denial and persecution and being cast out of all manner of places; it means obedience to Him and a light-hearted willingness to suffer all manner of things for His sake and the Gospel.

For some, perhaps many, this matter of being called to self-denial, suffering, and persecution may appear to be an unbelievable claim because, it is said, so few clergy follow this way in our time. That objection reflects an attitude that is strongly allied with worldly standards and where the objection can be seen to have some validity on whatever grounds, it stands as a confirmation of my point: where there is no self-denial and suffering for the Gospel's sake, there is no calling.

We are not called to proclaim or promote ourselves or the churches, although many have done so and continue to do so. One of the clearest marks of infidelity to God's call is the use of the calling for self-promotion and self-aggrandizement. Here, too, we have to admit that the ranks of the clergy include those who use the churches and the calling as a means to advance their own interests and ambitions. There is no justification in the clergy calling for egoism, narcissism, or self-aggrandizement. The ambitious who seek to promote themselves have sold out God's call and calling. Richard Neuhaus has correctly stated the issue:

> From ambition we should draw back as from lethal poison. But it is countered, we should be ambitious for doing good. If the attainment of some position of greater power and influence can increase the good we can do, what could possibly be wrong with that? It is a seductive line of reasoning. It is the reasoning that underlies the corruption of careerism in the ministry, that makes it almost automatic that successful ministries move on to successively larger churches until they are crowned by executive posts, honorary doctorates, and the bishop's mitre.[1]

In contrast, a mark of faithfulness to the sacred call is a life lived in self-sacrifice and selflessness for the sake of Christ and

---

1   Richard John Neuhaus, *Freedom for Ministry*, p. 212.

His Gospel. It is unlikely that we clergy can ever remind ourselves enough that we are called to cast away all our self-interests, to diminish ourselves and deny ourselves while giving the glory to God in Christ. "For what we preach is not ourselves, but Jesus Christ as Lord"! (2 Cor. 4:5)

The third testing that faces us again and again is our steadfastness in believing in God and serving God in Christ. In a memorable phrase, Karl Barth expressed this by saying that we need always to have "a clear and direct apprehension of the truth that man is made to serve God and not God to serve man."[1] Getting this priority straight and keeping it straight is incumbent upon us. How straight and reliable are we? There can be no dismissing, qualifying, or tampering with what we are called to be. Nor can there be any quick and easy brushing aside what will be our lot in this calling. Those who preach Christ's Gospel will not have an easy or peaceful time in this world. And that, too, is a mark and measure of our calling.

The Impossibility and Necessity of It All

Of course we are called to an impossible calling, humanly speaking. Moreover, the enormity of the task is crushing. Karl Barth aptly stated the issue: "As ministers we ought to speak of God. We are human, however, and so cannot speak of God. We ought therefore to recognize both our obligation and our inability and by that very recognition give God the glory. This is our perplexity. The rest of our task fades into insignificance in comparison."[2]

Our perplexity is the frustration of being human and being called into the service of God. We come to this calling with the disturbing awareness that we shall always be less than completely faithful; that we shall often be less than we ought to be or need to

---

1   Karl Barth, *The Word of God and the Word of Man.* New York: Harper and Row, 1957 edition, p. 196.

2   *Ibid.*, p. 186.

be; and that we shall frequently let our Lord down. Yet we must continue holding on and going on in His name. Why? Because we have been called! In *Brother to a Dragonfly*, Will Campbell describes a Baptist preacher whose career had been a dazzling success by the standards of the church and the world. He was also a person of monumental contradictions whose life seldom squared with the Gospel that he preached. One day Campbell asked, "'Why did you ever decide to be a Baptist preacher?' He looked puzzled and not just a little hurt. He pondered my question for a long time … Finally he looked me straight in the eye and answered my question: "'Cause I was *called*, you goddam fool!'"[3]

St. Paul knew only too well the paradox and the frustrations of being called to this impossible calling and in that wonderful, illuminating fourth chapter of the Second Letter to the Corinthians, he drew the conclusion on our plight: "It is the God who said, 'Let light shine out of the darkness,' who has shone in our hearts to give the light of the knowledge of the glory of God in the face of Christ. But we have this treasure in earthen vessels, to show that the transcendent power belongs to God and not to us. We are afflicted in every way, but not crushed; perplexed, but not driven to despair; persecuted, but not forsaken; struck down, but not destroyed; … " "So we do not lose heart. … We look not to the things that are seen but to the things that are unseen." (2 Cor. 4:6–9; 16; 18) Because we've been called!

A Path to Holiness

One more thing remains to be said about living this calling and that concerns the character of our life. In this age, many clergy and church leaders would have us think that to speak of holiness as a characteristic of our calling is to engage in some kind of unrealistic and hopelessly arcane spirituality that is best left to the past. On these terms, it usually is suggested that our character is

---

3   Will D. Campbell, *Brother to a Dragonfly*. New York: The Seabury Press, 1977, p. 173.

best formed and attested to through training and education in a multitude of "disciplines." We are urged and usually required by the churches to be instructed in the academies and seminaries and graduate schools and now also in "clinical" training, counseling, therapy, group dynamics, human potential skills, management by objectives, and countless other disciplines and methods. Passing through a maze of certification requirements for all kinds of "specialties" is said to characterize a competent pastor and many clergy offices are festooned with framed certificates and diplomas. To hang our calling by these threads is to hang by some very thin threads indeed. Our characters ought to be formed and "qualified" in another way, but seldom is any attention given to the spiritual discipline for holiness. Richard Neuhaus's pithy suggestion turns us in the right direction: "If the wall of the pastor's office is to make a declaration worthy of our calling, let it display a simple cross or crucifix."[1]

It is no exaggeration to say that one distinctive characteristic of so many clergy now is lack of spiritual formation and development. It is exhibited in a restless kind of hopelessness, in a frenzy of activities, and in a disturbing inability to wait upon God. The results of this fatal shortcoming are dejected, discouraged, lost, and broken clergy, wandering about in the wilderness of society. It is no wonder that there is so much unease and perpetual moving from parish to parish and place to place among so many clergy. Lacking in spiritual formation, they do not know how to trust God and wait for God, turning instead to one "trend" after another for some new and as yet undiscovered way to make all things right and well. No satisfactory answers will be found in the culture or any new form of "self-realization." Things will not be right and well apart from an abiding trust in God and a steadfast practice of living in the spirit and waiting upon God.

Of course the path to holiness is a perilously narrow one from

---

1   Richard John Neuhaus, *Freedom for Ministry*, p. 57.

which it is ever so easy to slip off into the way of self-delusion and deception. In the end, however, there is no escaping the matter of our character and what it counts for in living this calling. We need to get on the path to holy living and stay on it to the end. To strive for that "holiness without which no one will see the Lord" (Heb. 12:14) is the spiritual discipline of our calling; it involves a lifelong exercise of re-forming our character; of course, it is the most important "discipline" of all. The re-forming begins with our outward acts and deeds and then proceeds to our inmost ways. Those steps, in order, are crucial, as John Henry Newman pointed out in saying, "Outward acts, done on principle, create inward habits."[2] Cardinal Newman remains one of our truest and most reliable guides to the spiritual discipline of holy living. Again and again he emphasized the importance of steadfast, repeated acts of obedience to God: "Is not holiness the result of many patient, repeated efforts after obedience, gradually working on us, and first modifying and then changing our hearts?"[3]

The re-forming of our characters proceeds in many ways. Foremost among the means of grace is the holy eucharist, and a regular, disciplined eucharistic life is the foundation and sustenance of all Christian living. Then, whether it be by following such guides as Thomas A. Kempis' *The Imitation of Christ*, the inspired *Spiritual Exercises* of Ignatius Loyola, or William Law's *A Serious Call to a Devout and Holy Life*, it is incumbent upon us to concentrate upon our spiritual direction, turning aside from all the other directions of our age. It is time to stop escaping; we need to get on the path to holy living and stay on it to the end.

Three final things need to be recovered—or discovered—in order to take us on the path toward holiness. First, a distinctive attribute of our character by which we ought to be identified in this calling is that we are the ones who worry about salvation. This

---

2 John Henry Newman, *Parochial and Plain Sermons*. San Francisco: Ignatius Press, 1987 ed., p. 10.

3 *Ibid.,* p. 11.

---

is to say, we are committed to worrying about the salvation of all those who cross our path as well as those committed to our care by the churches. The holy pastor is one who endlessly worries about the salvation of all those souls. Together with the worrying comes the agonizing discipline of praying without ceasing for salvation. The worrying and the praying are always joined together. It is a spiritual discipline of our calling.

Also to be recovered—or discovered—for the re-forming of ourselves is that ancient and sacred Hebrew characteristic of the rabbis, the devout study of the scriptures. For the old rabbis, Torah study was the most sacred and holy of endeavors, to be pursued with the utmost attention and devotion. No other endeavor was to be given a prior claim upon their time and attention. Here was a spiritual discipline of the highest order that required diligent tending throughout a lifetime. How could we have missed it? Yet, this discipline is more ignored than honored or practiced by many clergy now. "Training" in "the strange new world within the Bible" as Karl Barth named it, is indispensable for our calling. If we practice it, the pursuit of the scriptures as a lifetime discipline of devotion shall work its way upon us, re-forming us into more faithful disciples drawn closer to the Word of God.

Finally, and most important of all, the path to holiness is that of facing the Cross and bearing our crosses. To face the Cross of Jesus Christ is to acknowledge as never before its supreme importance. That importance is so because His Cross is different from all other crosses even as it makes sense of all the others. In His Cross is embodied the fullness of God, which is surely to mark its difference and its surpassing importance. In it we come to know all that we need to know about God.

In one of his sermons, Cardinal Newman said that "there is but one Cross and one character of mind formed by it."[1] In that illuminating phrase, Newman draws attention to both the absolute

---

1   *Ibid.*, p. 1473.

distinctiveness of the Cross and its formative way for us. We face the Cross to learn of God and to know how to bear our crosses. The re-forming of ourselves comes by way of the Cross, which is the way of giving up ourselves and letting go of ourselves and all the things of this world. The extent to which we can let go is the extent to which we are on the path to holiness, taking our crosses and bearing them in His name to the end. That end is set before us as the conclusion that we too are called to preach as Christ crucified and risen. The path to holiness lies in asking "God for the grace to persevere for the few hours of our life under the cross of Christ, ... until we too can return our poor souls into the hands of God: crucified and thus liberated for eternal life."[2]

---

2   Karl Rahner, *The Priesthood*. New York: The Seabury Press, 1973, p. 237.

CHAPTER 3

Success and the Sacred Calling

For Christ did not establish and institute the ministry of proclamation to provide us with money, property, popularity, honor or friendship, nor to let us seek our own advantage through it; but to have us publish the truth freely and openly, rebuke evil, and announce what pertains to the advantage, health, and salvation of souls.[1]

– MARTIN LUTHER

WHENEVER WE BEGIN TO THINK ABOUT OUR SUCCESS, WE'D BETTER watch out, because that is when we're in trouble. We're in trouble because there is no success in our calling; there is only failure as the world measures success and failure. Our grade is always going to be F if we are faithful and true to our calling.

This seemingly implausible and impossible tension between success and failure is the substance of all sacred ministry. We have

---

1   *Luther's Works*, ed. Jaroslav Pelikan. St. Louis: Concordia Publishing House, 1956, vol. 21, p. 9.

been called to serve God through Jesus Christ and as much as anything else that means we are going to be failures in terms of how the world measures success and failure. Much of the church and the church's leadership measures success and failure on the world's terms and in worldly terms. But there is a distinctive guideline set for us and our calling: The greater the degree to which we become successful on those terms, the more we have sold out and become unfaithful to our calling. And the more that we seem to stumble and fail is probably one of the more reliable signs that we are becoming faithful at last. Our grade is always going to be F when we are faithful to our calling.

To be sure, this is a seemingly impossible, some would say a quixotic standard, but the biblical tradition that guides us and gives us the measure of all things is unanimous: only in needfulness, powerlessness, and a meek and lowly presence do we see the salvation of God. Our sacred calling is not an invitation to success, recognition, and well-being as the world thinks of those things. Here, then, is a fateful tension and conflict, the conflict between our calling and being successful in the eyes of the church and the world.

Success: The Beguiling Snare

The manifold temptations to think more highly of ourselves than of our calling beset clergy all too frequently. Augustine described our human nature so well when he wrote of himself: "In this was my sin, that not in God but in his creatures, in myself and others, did I seek pleasure, honors, and truth."[1] It is not that we simply want to honor God's call. It is also so easy for us to fall into the trap of equating our ideas of accomplishment with that call. We can never be certain; indeed, we are always uncertain about whether we are fulfilling God's call in a faithful way. We live in a

---

1   St. Augustine, *Confessions*, Book I, Chapter 20, in *Basic Writings of St. Augustine*, ed. Whitney J. Oates. Grand Rapids: Baker Book House, 1980.

society that surrounds us with a dazzling assortment of goals and measurements of accomplishment. Numbers of people baptized, confirmed, added to the membership rolls; numbers of pledges made and paid; numbers of children in Sunday School; numbers of youth in groups; numbers at Sunday services; numbers of picnics, bazaars, fairs; numbers, numbers, numbers. And real estate: the parish's plant, its size and development, "moving up" to larger or more stable or more promising parishes. A continuous assortment of aims, goals, and standards impinges upon us and competes for our life and work. There are intense, often compelling pressures to begin thinking that unless we measure up to the standards of the world, then we are failing to fulfill our calling. First, there are usually pressures from our parish councils to "get the numbers up" and bring in more "big contributors." Sometimes these pressures are subtle and implicit; sometimes they are bluntly laid upon us. Then there are the pressures from the church leadership—the regional, state, or diocesan office; the national offices; in some cases even the pension funds exert pressure. (Be a success or your pension will be negligible!) And certainly there are peer pressures and the images of successful clergy that impinge upon our self-image.

The striving to move up to larger or more established parishes embodies the stereotypical images of success and reward to which we can fall prey. These include better salaries, better houses, more reimbursed expenses, more assistance with administrative chores (so that we have time for "service"), recognition (at last!) of our capabilities and perhaps even notice and influence in the regional and national councils of the church. The images and rewards of success can become all-consuming as well as self-deceiving. We are all too susceptible to the desires for a better life in this world. As Augustine said, "in myself and others, did I seek pleasure, honors, and truth." The beguiling lure of success embodies self-deception and distortion about our calling, and the more we become attracted to images of success, the more difficult it becomes to perceive the truth and profess the truth. Whether it be the fears of losing our parish posts, or having our salaries frozen, or suffering crucial defeats in church council meetings, the pressures to be successful distort, disrupt, and destroy our professing and our profession. It is relatively easy to rationalize the images of success and begin seeing them as the fulfillment of our calling. The propensities of our minds to distort and rationalize are infinite and amazing. The way in which we perceive and think about our calling and career is so easily ensnared by the lure of success. We are not effective or useful unless we are winning, whether it be winning the votes of the church council, the search committee, or the election to a higher office. We are failures if the numbers are not increasing. Successful clergy are those whose numbers and leadership are so impressive that they are beckoned to higher and better parishes. Even more successful are those who get elected to higher offices— district superintendents, synod presidents, bishops!

This is the place for a short digression to consider those elections and their effects upon our calling. Elections to higher office are one of the most corrupting influences to which clergy are susceptible in our time. In the Middle Ages, the sale of appointments to higher clerical posts became the source of substantial corruption and abuse to the point that clergy were encumbering themselves with heavy loans to purchase additional appointments and waivers from the limitations on the number of appointments that could be held at one time. Different but no less awful patterns of corruption and corruptibility can be observed now in terms of the electoral process and its effects upon the characters and practices of clergy. Clergy who aspire to be synod presidents or conference presidents or bishops often expend the greatest energies of their lives in pursuit of such posts. Campaigns involving self-promotion, the making of deals, and strenuous efforts by candidates to ingratiate themselves with all manner of folk have come to characterize church elections. Not surprisingly, those who excel at this kind of campaigning get elected. Even less surprising is the result: that many of those so elected turn out to be such bad pastors and shepherds. The capabilities and traits needed to win elections are hardly those characteristic of a good shepherd. To win elections involves placing that goal above all other goals. More often than not, to win elections involves using people to get votes without regard to principles or moral conduct. More often than not, to win elections involves practicing self-deception in order to deceive others. And campaigning to win elections inevitably involves large measures of self-advertisement and self-aggrandizement. These attributes are not those of our sacred calling! Certainly they are the opposites of self-renunciation and giving up ourselves and being outcasts who are persecuted for the sake of Christ and the Gospel.

Like Richard Nixon, who made a career of running for offices but performed in a far less exemplary way once he won those offices, many clergy have invested their lives in pursuit of higher posts, gaining them at the expense of self and others. It ought to be expected that the elective process will give the churches self-centered leaders, for the process requires success-seeking, self-aggrandizing candidates who will arrange any deal or ingratiate themselves for high prices in order to win.

More fundamentally, the electoral process has no place in the churches because it has no warrant in the Scriptures and is antithetical to the biblical tradition. The Hebrew Bible presents a long tradition of Yahweh's intervention in history and choosing of His leaders and spokesmen. The lot was cast as a way to insure that people not manipulate and that God's choice be clear. (See 1 Sam. 14:41; Prov. 16:33.) It has been a long time since that biblical procedure has been used by any church in selecting its leaders. With the exception of some Mennonite communities, the biblical standard has been ignored and rejected. It's time for churches to turn away from campaigns and candidates and elections in favor of the biblical way. "The lot is cast into the lap; but the whole disposing thereof is of Jehovah." (Prov. 16:33) To do so would not produce poorer selections than those the churches have made in the past. To do so might see the first blessing poured out upon the churches since those early days. Many words have been uttered about the role of the Holy Spirit in episcopal and synodical elections. They generally add up to bad theology and hypocritical actions. The elective process embodies the aims and goals of worldly success and striving to achieve power and honor for ourselves and our ideologies. The simple standard of casting lots eliminates all that and puts the choice into the unexpected, unpredictable, uncontrolled realm of the Spirit of God. Casting lots for higher clerical offices would save many clergy from a lifetime of unworthy pursuits in which they abandon their call and the calling.

Turning now from elections to the matter of success in general, the clergy success ladder is an ascending one and to move up on that ladder is regarded as being essential; not to do so is to be a failure. The marks of failure include declining numbers, controversies, dissensions, and "setbacks." In the eyes of the world, failures are bad and only successes are worthwhile. Insofar as we come to appropriate the images and ideals of success, so we become indistinguishable from the world. And that is a problem for us. It is a problem because we were never called to mimic the world or adore the world or sell our souls to the world. We were called to serve Jesus Christ and to profess His Lordship over all creation. Nevertheless, the lure and temptations of the world's glitter remain. And foremost among the measures of success is the possession and exercise of "power."

Power: The Icon of Our Age

"Power" has become *the* icon and idol of our age. Everywhere and in every place the pursuit of power is now paramount. Which is to say that self-seeking has once again established the agenda and mission for society. Character formation is guided and measured by the propensity for power and the proximity to power. In the churches the pursuit of power has become just as visible and strong as in politics, the universities, or medicine and the law. The pursuit of power and the exercise of power over others is an identifying mark of the churches. Both clergy and laity have become ensnared in the pursuit of power—the laity in terms of governing parishes, bossing the clergy, and "empowering" themselves; the clergy in pursuing larger, more influential parishes and higher posts in the ecclesiastical structure. In the United States all but the Roman Catholic clergy have been subjected to being held hostage and captive to a ruling laity because of the pervasiveness and influence of congregational government. "Firing the preacher" is an established and honored part of the warp and woof of American Protestantism. The exercise of power is uppermost in the minds and wills of many laity and is epitomized in the widely held principle that "because we pay the clergy, we have the final say." Power is having the final say about things and controlling things, and taken on those terms, the church is one more institution for power-seeking and power-playing people.

When we turn to the clerical side of this matter seldom is the pursuit of power more visible and corrupt than in the intense campaigns and maneuvers for election and appointment to higher ecclesiastical offices. While the response to God's call and ordination may come about in many different and even seemingly implausible ways, one irrevocable requirement of that response has always been a commitment to self-denial and the end of all self-seeking pursuits of power, honor, and fortune. Our Lord emphatically made it clear that those called to follow Him would have to give up everything else.

In sharp opposition to that call, many clergy can be observed pursuing parishes and ecclesiastical offices with an incredible fervor of self-seeking and self-promotion. Self-denial, sacrifice, and humility have been pushed aside in favor of personal profits, security, self-aggrandizement, and the wielding of power. True to the twisted character of all hypocrisy, such pursuits inevitably are carried out in our Lord's name. Whether it be the pastor who contrives to garner splendid houses, shiny automobiles, and a multitude of "gifts" or one who cleverly plots and develops a career path that leads directly to a bishop's throne, the results are the same:

a life of corruptive hypocrisy that yields rotten fruit. We need to see them for what they are and begin naming their names. We need to have the clear vision and plain speaking shown by Annie Eliza Hicks in Clarence Major's novel, *Such Was the Season*.[1] Annie Eliza tells about her successful preacher son, Jeremiah: "Jeremiah's driveway was full of Cadillacs and Mercedes-Benzes and they had them parked all up and down the block. Four of them Cadillacs belonged to Jeremiah. He always say they belong to the church and to God but I never saw the church or God driving them." Yes indeed! God never drove all those Cadillacs!

The attractions of power and the pursuit of power collide with everything that is our calling. Power, which is having the say about everything and controlling everything, is judged unanimously throughout the Bible: only in needfulness, powerlessness, and righteousness do we see the salvation of God. In *The Mighty From Their Thrones*, James Walsh has given us a much needed and definitive study of power in the biblical tradition.[2] That tradition is best summarized in Walsh's apt translation of Luke 1:52: "He puts down the mighty from their thrones and exalts the lowly." Now that is about as decisive a condemnation of power as you can find anywhere. Certainly it is one that has much to tell us about power in the churches. How we evaluate ourselves and our faithfulness to our calling is to be measured by the inspired, definitive standards given to us in the biblical tradition. On those terms, it is clear that power seeking, self-seeking, and success-seeking have no place in our calling and ordination to serve God. The seeking of power and success is judged harshly and dealt with decisively by our God whose justice is everlasting. Justice and righteousness are among the most prominent and pronounced traits of God as given to us throughout the biblical tradition. And according to that tradition, God wills that power shall be taken from those who have sought and exercised it. The

---

1   Clarence Major, *Such Was the Season*. San Francisco: Mercury House, 1987, p. 19.
2   J.P.M. Walsh, *The Mighty From Their Thrones*. Philadelphia: Fortress Press, 1987.

power shall be taken from them and given to the meek, the lowly, and the powerless. Because it is the Gospel's judgment upon the worldly power and powers and power seekers, we need to test them all. But for us clergy especially we must test our characters and the characters of all those who seek to lead the churches.

The Conflict Between Success and Our Calling

Can we pursue success and remain faithful to our calling? No! We cannot do so in terms of the world's ideas of success. To remain faithful to our calling, it is necessary to renounce success and promotion of ourselves and aggrandizement of ourselves. To remain faithful to our calling is to be devoted to truth, purity, and love of Christ. Needless to say, there is an enduring conflict between this seemingly impossible calling and the attractions of the world. Earlier in this chapter I mentioned St. Augustine, who resolved this conflict by seeing our continuously self-seeking and self-deceiving human natures corrected and saved by divine grace and guidance. Martin Luther saw the matter somewhat differently; human life is simultaneously righteous and sinful, being made righteous by faith in Jesus Christ and yet entirely sinful in ourselves. Whatever our theological convictions in this regard, we are stuck with the conflict. It is part of our calling, and to evade it or ignore it is to lessen our calling. How we live with it is more important than whether we think we have conquered it or accommodated it or been defeated by it.

How we come to live with our identity and our calling can make all the difference for us and our calling. One of the best examples to guide us in this regard is Cardinal Newman. It was in an especially dark and perplexing time of his life, after he had left the Anglican church as a matter of conscience and had been received into the Roman Catholic Church, where he met considerable suspicion and jealousy, that Newman wrote:

God has created me to do Him some definite service; He has committed some work to me which He has not committed to another. I have my mission—I may never know it in this life, but I shall be told it in the next. I am a link in a chain, a bond of connection between persons. He has not created me for nothing. I shall do good, I shall do His work. Therefore, I will trust Him. Whatever, wherever I am.[1]

Much of the time we find it difficult and perplexing to know our mission. The conflict between success and our calling can distort our perception and involve self-deception. Often, like Newman, we simply do not know; but how we live with this darkness will make all the difference. Newman's clear and enduring theological conviction rings true: That God has created us to do something to which He has entrusted no others and although we may never know the purpose in this life, yet we shall trust Him.

The seemingly infinite gulf between the success of the world and our calling brings us to the center of everything about our calling, which is the matter of taking Jesus seriously and following after Jesus. As Mother Teresa said so eloquently: "We are not here for the work, we are here for Jesus. All we do is for Him. We are first of all religious; we are not social workers, not teachers, not nurses or doctors ... Without Jesus our life would be meaningless, incomprehensible; Jesus explains our life."[2] Jesus is the truth to which we must turn as we are beset by the perplexities of this lifelong conflict and tension. The best thing we can do is to keep reminding ourselves that more often than not we shall be perplexed by this conflict. Moreover, the more that we struggle with it, the more we probably shall fail. There are two points to be made

---

1   John Henry Newman, *Meditations and Devotions*. Wheathampstead, U.K.: Anthony Clarke Books, 1964, pp. 6–7.

2   Quoted in Edward LeJoly, *Mother Teresa of Calcutta*. San Francisco: Harper & Row, 1977, pp. 5–6.

about this: The first is that being perplexed is the enduring state of our humanity, which I am confident shall be made clear when we finally come face to face with our Lord. The second point is that to fail, as the world defines failure, is the essence and nature of our calling. Our Lord often said that only those who lose their lives *for His sake* will ever find them. The failure to succeed is an innate part of our calling. How we live with that failure is the measure of our faithfulness to the calling.

What Then Shall Come of Our Calling?

Having arrived at this point, I can easily imagine some objections and even despair upon the part of some, if not most readers. "What shall we do?" "If what you are saying is authentic, then we can't do anything!" To that (with my fellow preacher Will Campbell) I say, Yes, indeed! That's the point. Nail that down. Do nothing! Be somebody! Be a disciple of Jesus!

In his autobiography, Will Campbell refers to Thomas Merton's advice that we need to stop worrying about what to do and begin trying to follow Jesus and then we'll know what to do. What is involved here is clarity of truth, wisdom wrested out of struggle, and the simplicity of the pure in heart. What shall become of our calling is in God's hands and what that may be may never become very clear to us in this life. As Jonathan Swift once remarked with his characteristic irony: "Neither did our Savior think it necessary to explain to us the nature of God, because I suppose it would be impossible without bestowing on us other Faculties than we possess at present."[3]

What shall become of us and our calling in this world is not very much revealed to us. There are occasional flashes of light and glimpses of insight, just as we have been given the gift of our calling

---

3 Jonathan Swift, *Gulliver's Travels and Selected Writings*. London: Nonesuch Press, 10th printing, 1979, p. 410.

and told what to expect of it. Such a glimpse has come to me often in a remarkable book, *Morte D'Urban*, written by J.F. Powers.[1] Again and again I have found myself returning to *The Death of Urban* for over fifty years. It is a book that never fails to cheer me and make me laugh when nothing else can do so, perhaps because I see so much of myself in it. I want to describe the story briefly because it embodies such a sound theological perception of the church, the clergy, and the mysterious ways of God.

Morte D'Urban is the story of Father Urban, who as a young boy in southern Illinois was recruited for the novitiate of the Order of St. Clement by a dashing traveling evangelist, Father Placidus. To say the least, the Clementines were one of the most bedraggled and forgotten of all the religious orders. They not only didn't know a good thing when they saw it, but they usually managed to turn a good thing into a disaster. Father Urban's Pastor, Monsignor Morez, had referred to the Clementines as the *Rinky Dinks*, as he tried to dissuade the boy from joining them. Nevertheless, like many of us, Father Urban knew that he had been called, even as he came to understand that God uses some pretty unusual ways to attract those chosen for this sacred calling. Father Urban's story is one involving a lifelong struggle to be faithful to that call while being beset with the lures of success.

In the years following his assignment to the Clementines' traveling staff, Father Urban's abilities as a preacher, evangelist, and fund raiser developed immensely. His popularity with parishes, schools, and civic organizations increased each year. But at age fifty-four, just when he was poised to "land some big fish" for the Clementines, Urban is transferred to the Order's newest white elephant, an abandoned sanitarium in northern Minnesota. However, even this seemingly ludicrous setback and the inane, slapdash ways of Urban's new superior, Father Wilfred ("Wif"), are surmounted as Urban manages to make something out of the situation. In

---

1   J.F. Powers, *Morte D'Urban*. Garden City: Doubleday and Company, Inc., 1962.

weekly preaching assignments Urban builds support for the Clementines from the surrounding parishes and in the second year all of his efforts come to fruition when a benefactor's gifts transform St. Clement's Hill into an enterprising religious center, complete with a new nine-hole golf course. The former white elephant becomes the shining star of the Clementines with its full program of retreats and popular new facilities. Then Urban is hit in the head and knocked senseless by a golf ball driven by the Bishop of the Diocese. Shortly thereafter Urban is selected as the new Provincial of the Clementines! A crippled and faltering Father Urban has been elevated to the pinnacle of the Order. Once back in Chicago as Father Provincial, Urban is beset by continuing headaches and attacks that come on like two sections of a train approaching in succession. He is "not well." And in his first year as Provincial, the headquarters lease is lost, the weekly radio program is lost, and even the beloved elm trees at the Novitiate have to be cut down because of blight. Urban becomes another casualty. The bright and shining plans and dreams of his lifetime have been broken to nothing by a stray golf ball! Surely this was a cruel turn of fate and a grotesque joke. Or was it the final confirmation of a different plan? The inescapable suggestion of J.F. Powers' book is that success in the church and its ministry has a strange and unusual way of ending up amounting to nothing. In other words, it just may be God's mysterious way not to suffer our successes and success-seeking, even at the expense of the church—or perhaps, for the sake of the church.

Ultimately what becomes of our calling is hidden in the decisive grasp of God. Our best strivings to succeed and our worst failings have a way of being turned upside down. Our best hopes and accomplishments for the church and ministry, like Urban's, have a way of ending up as senseless and our worst failures may be the only things counted worthwhile. This seemingly strange fate holds a clue for us; it is more than a clue—it is exactly what our Lord told us to expect from our calling.

CHAPTER 4

All Things To All People?

IN MORE THAN TWENTY-FIVE YEARS OF READING PARISH SEARCH COM-mittee profiles, I have noted a frequently expressed expectation that pastors ought to be "all things to all people." That impression has been confirmed by several clergy research studies.[1] Search committees routinely begin with the caveat that, of course, they realize no pastor can be all the things they want. And then frequently they proceed to write a list of specifications and qualifications that is remarkably close to that slogan. The slogan is far less a straw figure than one might surmise. One parish is searching for a strong preacher, skilled counselor, expert administrator, crisis manager, and community leader with an outgoing and pleasing personality. Another seeks an experienced pastor, administrator, fund raiser, teacher, and counselor who projects a youthful image. A third seeks

---

1 Jeffrey K. Hadden, *The Gathering Storm in the Churches*, Garden City: Doubleday and Co., 1969; Gerald J. Judd, Edgar W. Mills and Genevieve W. Burch, *Ex-Pastors*, Philadelphia: The Pilgrim Press, 1970; Thomas C. Campbell and Yoshio Fukuyama, *The Fragmented Layman*: An *Empirical Study of Lay Attitudes*, Philadelphia: The Pilgrim Press, 1970.

an impressive preacher who is also experienced in "church growth" (especially among the young), pastoral visitation, counseling, staff administration, ecumenical endeavors, and "renewal" of worship. This list of clergy "qualifications" and expectations is nearly endless. One recent profile I examined had developed so many traits and categories from a parish-wide survey that they probably needed a computer program to sort and compile all the factors and then correlate these with their various votes and preferences. Another recent search by an Episcopal bishop stated that he had failed to find anyone with all the "necessary qualifications" even after a nationwide computer scan of thousands of clergy.

From the clergy side, I have seen pastors work until they are shattered into a multitude of pieces trying to be all things to all people. Countless others, eager to move, attempt to portray themselves as the most complete and all-inclusive pastor alive, thereby promising what they are not and can never be in this life.

There is much to be said about what is wrong with the notion that clergy are called to be all things to all people. In the first place, that is the job description for a politician or a cruise ship social director, but it has nothing to do with this call and calling. Taken on the best of terms, the slogan suggests being committed to serving all the interests and needs of all people. In terms of God's call this immediately raises the theological problem of a vocation whose commitment is solely to serving human interests. All things to all people neither begins with God nor allows any place for God and so it cannot be applied to this calling.

Taken on its worst terms, the slogan entails a willingness to be anything or nothing, to be committed to anything or nothing, depending upon whom one is serving at the moment. Those who aim to be all things to all people are absolutely nothing themselves, standing only for their commitment to become anything for anyone. It is doubtful that such a person ever existed, but the slogan continues to lurk in many minds as the worthy model for clergy. Both those who advocate it and those who attempt to adhere to it have failed to understand the nature of this calling, for this calling stands for something but not everything. Whether it be the local search committee with its pages of demands and qualifications or the bishop who sought the universally perfect, all-experienced assistant, the root problem is far too much emphasis upon human interests, far too much trust in human abilities, and far too little emphasis upon God.

We were never called by God to be all things to all people—and nothing to God. Rather, we are called to live in this world while always looking beyond this world, speaking about what is to come in the time of God, which is to say, the Kingdom of God. The Kingdom message is our Lord's message and so it ought to be our message. In Julian Hartt's illuminating words: "Jesus Christ acknowledges the Kingdom of God as the sole and absolute warrant for his words and actions. It is not too much to say that on every page of the New Testament the truth of the Gospel of Jesus Christ is proved by an appeal to the Kingdom of God."[1] Our calling to speak of the Kingdom was aptly described by Luther when he said:

> The Word of God is not here to teach a maid or a servant how to work in the household and to earn his bread, nor a burgomaster how to rule, nor a farmer how to plow or make hay. In brief, it neither gives nor shows temporal goods for the preservation of this life, for reason has already taught all this to everyone. But it is intended to teach how we are to come to that other life.[2]

In speaking of this calling, Karl Barth pointed out the importance of getting our purpose clear: "It is evident that [people] do not need us to help them live, but seem rather to need us to help them die; for their whole life is lived in the shadow of death." Barth

---

1 Julian N. Hartt, *A Christian Critique of American Culture*. New York: Harper & Row, 1967, p. 167.
2 *Luther's Works*, vol. 21, p. 9.

then continued, speaking of the sudden recognition, often within death's shadow, that human life is "walking upon a ridge between time and eternity that is narrower than a knife-edge."[1] Thus when people come to us "they do not really want to learn more about living; they want to learn more about what is on the farther edge of living—God."[2] It may be that Barth expressed a bit too much confidence in the propensity of human interest for anything other than this world and this life. It is not that often, until perhaps the last hours, that most people show such interest if at all. Of course that situation emphasizes the purpose and need for this calling: "To announce what pertains to the salvation of souls."[3]

Instead of trying to be all things to all people, we are called to announce to all people that what matters is eternal life and the salvation of their souls. We are called to worry about the salvation of all those souls. We are called to sound the alarm again and again, telling all people that God bids them seek salvation even as He offers it to them. In a cogent summary, Luther said our task was to proclaim the truth freely and openly, to rebuke evil and to speak of the salvation of souls.[4] To do so is to testify for Christ with perpetual zeal.

Lest anyone think the need for this witness is irrelevant, the data of religious surveys ought to stand as sufficient evidence. In a 1968 study, for example, Glock and Stark reported that among church members studied, "a near majority reject such traditional articles of faith as Christ's miracles, life after death, the promise of the second coming, and the virgin birth."[5] That the "near majority" of church members hold these opinions, to say nothing of the

---

1   Karl Barth, *The Word of God and the Word of Man.* New York: Harper & Row, 1957, p. 188.

2   *Ibid.,* p. 189.

3   *Luther's Works,* vol. 21, p. 9.

4   *Ibid.*

5   Rodney Stark and Charles Y. Glock, *American Piety: The Nature of Religious Commitment.* Berkeley: University of California Press, 1968, p. 205.

---

unchurched, ought to show us the immense need for "publishing the truth freely and openly," to use Luther's phrase.

Neither the opinions of the world nor the churches and their majorities determine what we are called to proclaim. What those opinions do tell us, however, is what we are facing and what needs to be accomplished in both the world and the churches. Facing all those opinions, our calling is to proclaim "the gospel of the glory of Christ"(2 Cor. 4:4) and stick to that Gospel. Whether conversion takes place or not rests with God's providence and grace. The final reckoning of all remains with God, just as the final disposition of all souls is in God alone. Our calling is the much more modest one of delivering the message and holding steadfast to that message. "For necessity is laid upon me. Woe to me if I do not preach the gospel!" (1 Cor. 9:16)

There is a universality in our calling; however, it is not in being all things to all people, but in proclaiming Christ's Gospel to all people. We are called to all for the purpose of this solitary task of witness and proclamation in His name. This calling is that of the evangel who brings the salvation message to a church and a world that need to hear it and heed it, even as they deny it. The universal nature and dimension of this calling was described by the late Urban Holmes: "The priest speaks to the church for the God who speaks to the soul of every individual and community. The priest speaks for the church and to the church and the world."[6]

It is frequently argued in response to this claim of universality that all beliefs are equally valid and therefore the Christian message has no universal application or validity. The argument has been buttressed by assurances that the pluralism of this postmodern age has settled the matter once and for all. While this may well be yet another version of that ancient philosophical argument over the one and the many, what must be said about it in this instance is that

---

6   Urban T. Holmes III, *The Priest in Community*. New York: The Seabury Press, 1978, p. 156.

allegiance to wanton pluralism makes all belief meaningless. The validity of all ends up as the validity of none. The popular expression frequently stated in the argument over beliefs that "it makes no difference because it's the same God" not only begs the question but also contradicts the pluralistic principle. "Anything and everything because it is ultimately the same" is a striking piece of nonsense that circles back on itself and cancels out the entire argument. It makes no difference literally makes no difference, because it adds up to nothing. In this case, no difference equals nothing. By contrast, in the words of the Hartford Appeal, "Truth matters; therefore differences among religions are deeply significant."[1]

The significant differences in beliefs within religions and among religions are a matter for enduring exploration and conversation. But recognizing others, and even entering into open, sustained conversation with others, does not demand that we compromise or deny the belief and trust we hold in Jesus Christ as revealed Lord and Savior of all. Many are the distinctions to be made between the proximate visions of all religions (and within Christianity, among the churches) and the universal truth of God in Jesus Christ. Finally, the postmodern awareness of ambiguity and plurality does not let us off the hook or remove our essential decision any more than the awareness of other ages did for them.

"Truth matters" and for us in the call of this calling, God has placed His particular demand upon us. In this calling we are called to bring God's Gospel message to all people because it is about all and for all. "All things to all people?" Quite the contrary!—One thing to all people.

---

1   Peter L. Berger and Richard John Neuhaus, *Against the World for the World*. New York: The Seabury Press, 1976, p. 3.
